POCKET IMAGES

Around Launceston

Northgate Street in the 1930s. The tall building on the right was a common lodging house. It was one of the tallest buildings in the town but was demolished in 1957 after it was left empty for some time.

POCKET IMAGES

Around Launceston

Joan Rendell

NONSUCH

Miss Iris Gliddon is a well-known character in Launceston and is famed for her remarkable selection of postcards of churches. She has a picture postcard of every church in Cornwall and is now completing her collection of Devon church postcards.

First published 1997
This new pocket edition 2006
Images unchanged from first edition

Nonsuch Publishing Limited
The Mill, Brimscombe Port,
Stroud, Gloucestershire, GL5 2QG
www.nonsuch-publishing.com

Nonsuch Publishing is an imprint of Tempus Publishing Group

© Joan Rendell, 1997

Joan Rendell to be identified as the Author
of this work has been asserted in accordance with the
Copyrights, Designs and Patents Act 1988.

All rights reserved. No part of this book may be reprinted
or reproduced or utilised in any form or by any electronic,
mechanical or other means, now known or hereafter invented,
including photocopying and recording, or in any information
storage or retrieval system, without the permission in writing
from the Publishers.

British Library Cataloguing in Publication Data.
A catalogue record for this book is available from the British Library.

ISBN 1-84588-287-3

Typesetting and origination by Nonsuch Publishing Limited
Printed in Great Britain by Oaklands Book Services Limited

Contents

Introduction		7
1.	Commerce and Industry	9
2.	Town Pride and Joy	25
3.	Personalities	37
4.	The Changing Face of Town and Village	45
5.	The Farming Scene	67
6.	Occasions	71
7.	Sport and Leisure	77
8.	School Life	97
9.	Church and Chapel	107
10.	Around and About	115
Acknowledgements		128

Yeolmbridge had its worst floods when the River Attery burst its banks and water poured through the village, flooding several properties in June 1993.

Mrs Ruth Sleeman, chairman of trustees, unveiled a tablet in the recently opened exhibition & lecture room at Lawrence House Museum, April 1991. This was in recognition of the services given to the museum by the honorary curator Mr John Clarke over many years. On the right is the late Mr Eddie Dart, who succeeded Mr Clarke as honorary curator.

Introduction

Launceston, otherwise known as Dunheved, is a very historic and very interesting town with some delightful surrounding villages. That may sound excruciatingly banal but it is perfectly true. The town is steeped in history and its setting high on a hill is hard to beat. Once the pivot of a flourishing agricultural industry it is sadly no longer a market town, since it lost its cattle market several years ago, but it has had a rich industrial past. However, those industries on which it formerly relied have all gone, to be replaced by modern industry on two industrial estates. In the nineteenth century Newport was the centre of the woollen and tanning industries in the town; in the eighteenth and early nineteenth centuries the town was well-known for the making of straw hats; brewing and the wine trade were also busy and iron founders had plenty of work. The coming of the Bude Canal, although it terminated three miles from the town, brought the brickworks at Dutson. The traditional industries of milling and quarrying flourished but now most of the mills have been turned into dwellings or over to other commercial activity.

The town has changed considerably within the past two or more decades but its old world charm, its magnificent historical monuments and its aura of friendliness remain. I was born in the town and although for the greater part of my life I have lived in the adjoining parish of Werrington, my family roots in the town go back many generations.

Whether you live in Launceston or you are only visiting, the following selection of photographs will help you to capture some of its past atmosphere and set the scene for some of its glories which never change despite the passing of years.

Joan Rendell
Werrington, 1997.

The Cordery family of Werrington. Mr Cordery was a gardener at Polapit Tamar.

Opposite: Many of the photographs in this book were taken by Brimmell's photographic studio and this picture shows Brimmell's shop in Church Street in the 1930s. Brimmell's offered a diversity of services: hairdressing, newsagent, stationery and fancy goods, as well as the photography side of the business. Note the newspaper poster 'Italians enter Addis', a reference to the Italian campaign in Ethiopia in 1935.

One

Commerce and Industry

Commerce and industry in Launceston have changed very considerably over the years and most of the old family businesses have gone and the multiples have moved in. We now have out-of-town shopping and national names above shop fronts in The Square, but there are still plenty of small traders offering a personal and specialised service, just as there were years ago. Some of the photographs in this section will give an indication of how the cost of living has changed, but that is not peculiar to Launceston (or Lanson as it is correctly pronounced). Many older residents still refer to premises occupied by tradesmen in the past, such as Dunn's Corner or Doidge's shop at Newport. See, too, from the photographs, how the style of shop fronts have changed. Launceston has moved with the times but we must not deem it any the worse for that.

Dunn's East Cornwall Stores occupied a prominent position in The Square, known even today to older residents as Dunn's Corner. Elaborate window displays were always a feature. The shop is now Paxman's pharmacy.

Opposite above: Barriball's in Church Street was another well-known and very popular grocer's shop. It was famed far and wide for its own sausage recipe.

Opposite below: Treleaven's Corner, looking down Church Street. Treleaven's was the outfitter and ladies fashion retailer for a great many years. The premises are now the Halifax building society. Shuker and Reed, on the corner of Market Street was another popular grocery store and also a chemist. Shuker's were well-known for their Christmas gifts to customers, ranging from teapots and plates to clothes brushes, all bearing an advertisement for the firm, which are collectors' items today. The premises are now the Bristol & West building society.

GIVEN FREE
FARROW'S COOKED PEAS
FARROW'S
TOMATO KETCHUP
GIVEN FREE
FARROW'S COOKED PEAS
GIVEN FREE
FARROW'S
COOKED PEAS

SHUKER
REED

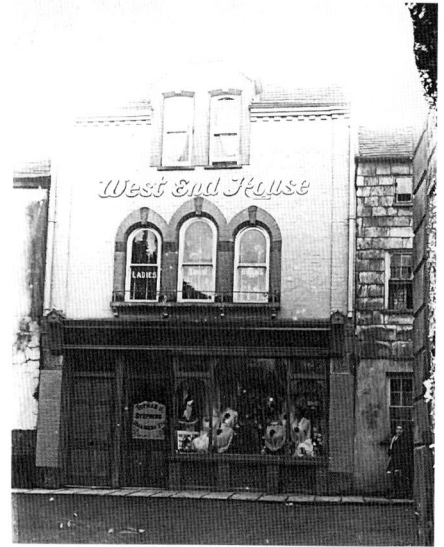

Above: Fitze the ironmonger was at one time a household name in Launceston. The last of the line, Mr Sidney Fitze, ran a successful ironmongery business in The Square, later taken over by Timothy White's and now housing Boots the chemist. The shop pictured here was in Westgate Street and shows Mr Sidney Fitze on the right with his father in the doorway of their shop.

Left: The Misses Tupman and Stephens establishment was a mecca for fashionable ladies. In the 1900s, the shop was in Westgate Street (now Windmill Patchworks and Cafe) but later moved to The Square.

A Christmas display at Messrs Folley and Reynolds shop in High Street. The shop specialised in the more unusual and exotic grocery items, especially at Christmas time. It was regarded as 'classy', if a mite expensive, but well worth it for the service and the range of goods offered. Note the crackers priced at 9 Er d. a box and large tins of biscuits at 1/1.

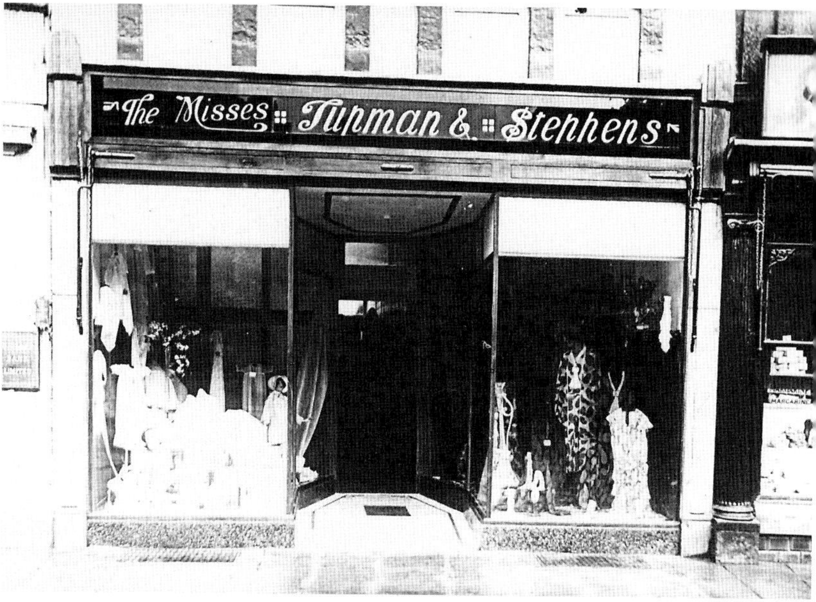
The Misses Tupman & Stephens

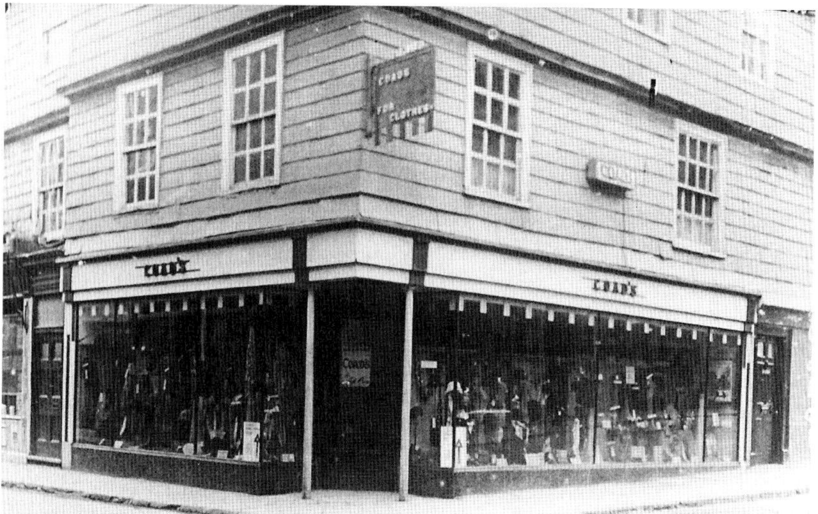
COAD'S
COAD'S

Right: Stanley Parsons bakers shop in Exeter Street was the place to go for a Christmas or wedding cake in the 1930s. Its smart art deco building was quite an innovation in the town.

Below: Robins bakery and tea shop in The Square was at one time a popular venue for meeting over a cup of tea or coffee, especially on market days, when it also served substantial midday meals for farmers and their families. The business later moved to Westgate Street. The building is now home to Thresher's Wine Store.

Opposite above: The Misses Tupman and Stephens shop in The Square. The latest in ladies' and children's fashions were always tastefully arranged in the windows but the proprietors made it a strict rule never to display lingerie in the window!

Opposite below: Coad's outfitters in the corner premises of Broad Street and Southgate Street provided affordable clothes for everyone, from working gear to a Sunday best suit or a fashionable small cloche hat in the 1930s. The shop is now the Oxfam charity shop.

Above left: Gillbard's was an ironmongery and saddlery business, but later, under the proprietorship of the late Mr Jack Rashley, became a seed and corn merchant. The premises in High Street are now occupied by Stokes, the greengrocers.

Above right: Hicks, boot and shoe retailer. Another well-established business now long gone.

Opposite: Williams the ironmonger in The Square sold scythe handles and many other items for use on the land. The upper facades of these buildings are little changed today but the shop fronts are completely different.

Telephone No. 8.   Telegrams: "TRELEAVEN, LAUNCESTON."

Treleaven & Son
Limited.

TAILORS & OUTFITTERS.

COSTUMIERS & MILLINERS.

LAUNCESTON.

Branch: 44, Fore Street, Callington.

Right: The Westgate Inn, *c.* 1900. The building looks very much smarter today. The west gate to the town originally stood nearby but was demolished in the early 1800s.

Below: The building of the Gillbard homes and centenary flats at Chapple in 1936. Mr C. H. Gillbard (shown holding a silver trowel) was a great benefactor to the town. The houses and flats which he provided are pleasant dwellings which are still occupied. In 1928 he presented the town council with robes for the aldermen and in 1937 gave a public park and sports ground (later known as Coronation Park) to the town.

Opposite: Treleaven's Corner. This well-known family run shop was the tailor and outfitter in the town. It was run by several generations of Treleavens before closing down in the 1980s. The premises are now the Halifax building society.

Left: The brickworks at Dutson. The manager of the brickworks stands proudly as another kiln is constructed.

Below: Bricks piled high for firing in one of the kilns.

Above: The brickworks at Dutson, 1930s. The brickworks evolved mainly to meet the needs of the Bude Canal, which terminated about 1 ¾ miles away at Druxton Wharf. It continued in production until the 1930s and in the 1960s its last remaining vestige, the chimney, was demolished.

Right: The demolition of the brickworks. A rueful manager surveys the havoc. Piles of drain pipes, made at the works, still remain stored in the niches.

Above: In 1910 people gathered at Treleaven's Corner to see the first tricycle driven through Launceston. Fashionable ladies even stood on Treleaven's balcony to watch the spectacle and children gazed wide-eyed. The local newspaper reporter was on hand with notebook (centre right) to record the event.

Excavating the site for the gasworks at Newport in the 1920s. The gasworks have long since closed and part of the site is now occupied by the Launceston Steam Railway.

Opposite below: The staff of J.B. Smith's garage in 1933. Pictured are Messrs T. Penny, B. Mills, B. Wilton, E. Phare, H. Nicholls, H. Fry, J. Anning and Misses B.Godbeer (now Mrs Jenkin) and J. Sillifant, office staff.

Preparing for the site for St Stephens church hall in the early 1900s.

Waiting for the last train at Egloskerry Station. This was one of the stations on the busy north Cornwall line. The famous *Atlantic Coast Express* from Waterloo to Padstow went through Egloskerry and the train was very popular with holidaymakers in the summer months. The line was closed under the 'Beeching axe' in 1964.

Two

Town Pride and Joy

The Castle and Southgate dominate Launceston, just as they have done for centuries. Add to that the splendid parish churches and it will be seen that the town has much of which to be proud. The photographs in this chapter detail the changes in even historic edifices over the years but basically they are still the same and even more cherished now than they were in years gone by, when conservation was an almost unknown word. No wonder the town is proud of its special glories.

An old engraving of Launceston Castle.

WITCHS TOWER LAUNCESTON

Launceston Castle and Lodge.

The Lodge and the entrance to the castle grounds in the early 1900s. The remains of the Witch's Tower are now mainly a grassy mound and can best be seen by taking a few steps into the entrance of a private car park on the south side of Western Road (opposite the tower remains).

Opposite above: The old well in the Castle Green, which was demolished in the early-nineteenth century.

Opposite below: An engraving of the Witch's Tower, Launceston Castle. The pond shown in this engraving no longer exists.

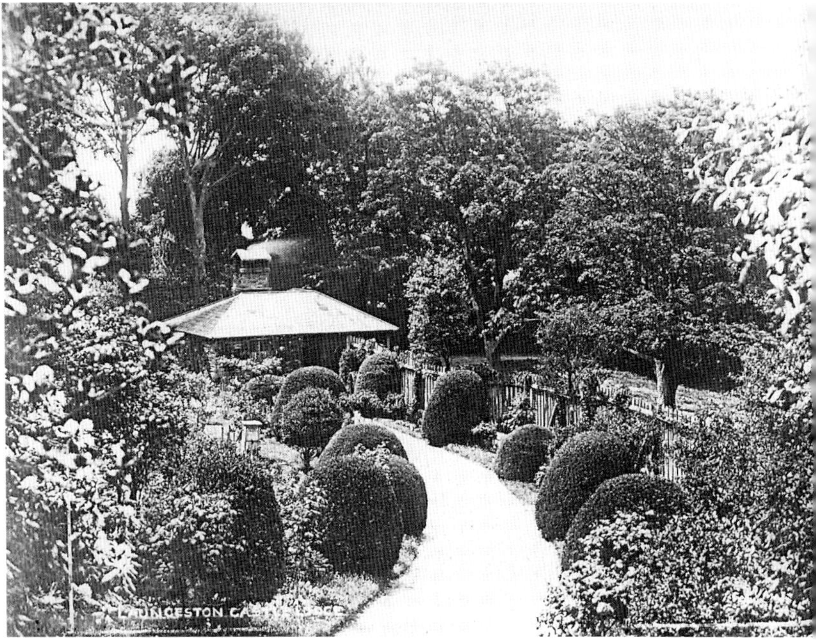
LAUNCESTON

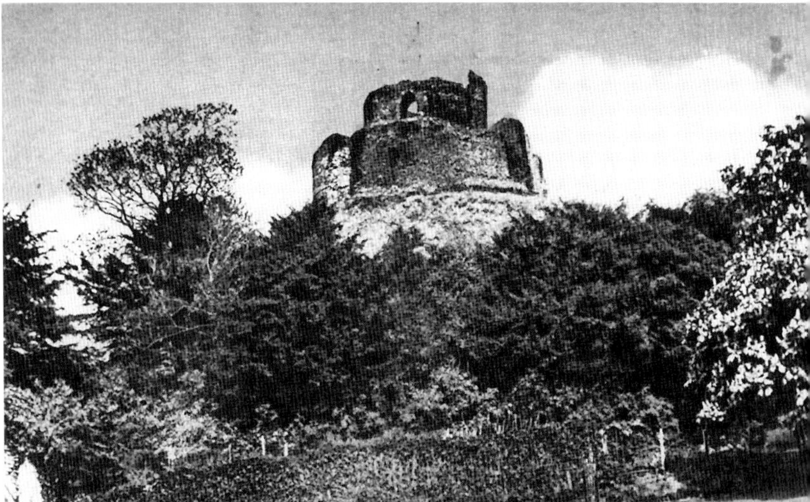

The south entrance to the castle in the early nineteenth century.

Opposite above: The Launceston Castle Lodge in 1908.

Opposite below: The castle seen from Castle Green in 1930. The fence, trees and bushes have now gone and the motte can be clearly viewed from the green.

Above: 'Paradise' in the 1930s. This was a delightful sun trap in the castle grounds and a pleasant place to sit, the seats were always occupied in fine weather. The sundial was a popular feature with children who loved trying to tell the time by it.

Left: The north gate of the castle, *c.* 1908. It is no longer overgrown and neglected as it was in those days.

Above: An old engraving of the South Gate to the town.

Right: A similar date to the engraving above taken from St Stephens Hill, showing the castle and St Mary Magdalene church.

Launceston Castle.

The castle grounds in the mid 1930s. The grounds were then lovingly tended by the custodian & gardener Mr R. Tolman, who lived with his wife and family in the lodge.

Launceston

The castle stands proudly above the Kensey Valley, railway stations and ancillary buildings.

The South Gate, which shows a turn into Madford Lane and a right into Exeter Street, before 1897.

The South Gate looking towards Race Hill in the 1930s.

The South Gate looking towards Church Street in the 1930s.

The famous sycamore tree which grew, without any visible sustenance, from the South Gate. It was removed in the 1980s and its removal raised a storm of protest from local residents.

The North Gate before demolition in the nineteenth century.

A painting of the South Gate by Wimbush in 1908.

In 1915 Launceston Town Hall was used as a military hospital tending men wounded in the First World War. A plaque on the wall in the town hall now commemorates that period in its history. Over 1,000 soldiers were treated there.

Castle Street (once described by John Betjeman as 'the finest Georgian street in Cornwall') as it was at the time of the Lawrence family who lived at Lawrence House, now the museum. The tree and houses near it have now gone.

Three

Personalities

They have all passed on but they all made their mark in their own little corner of Cornwall. They all contributed a great deal to their respective communities. Their contributions may seem minuscule in the context of world events but they are remembered still by many, even by those who never knew them, for their own little bit of Launceston history.

Caroline Jane Martin and Margaret Rundle standing outside No.11 Castle Street. On the left is the office of Thomas Pearse and his partner N.H.P. Lawrence, attorneys. It is now known as Trevean and is reputedly one of Launceston's old haunted houses. Caroline Jane Martin was the daughter of Miss Caroline Pearse's butler. Miss Pearse was daughter of Thomas Pearse and she built the house in front of which Caroline Pearse and Margaret Rundle are standing. After Mr and Mrs Martin died their daughter continued to live in No.11 and Margaret Rundle came to live there with her.

The Reed family of Weston, North Petherwin. They were a well-known farming family and Mr Reed built a farmhouse similar to his own at an adjoining farm, Cullacott, in the parish of Werrington.

Mr Ephraim Jenkin of South Petherwin, a well-known local figure.

Mrs Ephraim Jenkin.

The father and grandfather of Miss Mabel Maddever of South Petherwin. Miss Maddever, now 93 years of age, was a well-known and popular schoolmistress in her home parish of South Petherwin and later in Launceston.

Miss Emma Tingcombe, later Mrs Frederick Culley, c. 1850. Miss Tingcombe was the first woman appointed in an executive capacity at the White Hart Hotel, Launceston.

Employees at Penheale (home of Col. Colville), Egloskerry. Left to right: Mr Donald, Miss Donald, Mr Moffat Snr.

Mr and Mrs Francis Squire Stenlake of North Petherwin in the year of their marriage at St Stephens church, Launceston in April 1922. Mrs Stenlake was born Mary Margaret Facy of Rockwell, St Stephens.

Left: Miss Mary Ellen Wright, known to her family as 'Pops'. She was a familiar figure in Newport, Launceston. As a dressmaker, she was much in demand and made a number of wedding dresses for brides at St Stephens church.

Below: Mr and Mrs Percy Cory and granddaughter Uralie at the Well of St Keyne, near Liskeard in 1932. Mr Cory was well-known over a wide area as an insurance agent and will always be remembered as a man who would do a kindness for everybody.

Above: The wedding of Mr and Mrs Owen Jenkin at South Petherwin. Mrs Jenkin, *née* Squance, was, like her husband, a member of a well-known South Petherwin family. Mr Squance, the bride's grandfather, seen in the photograph, was in his nineties at the time of the wedding.

Right: Miss Lizzie Ann Furse was a teacher at Werrington School in the early 1900s.

Left and far left: The Misses Sloman who were both good singers and attended Boyton Methodist chapel, where their talents were highly prized. The sisters were popular for their singing duets. Miss Polly Sloman was the infants' teacher at Boyton School.

The Horrell family of Boyton. This photograph was taken on the occasion of the golden wedding of Mr and Mrs J.T. Horrell (seated). Their children (standing) are, left to right: Charles, Millicent, Archie and William. William served with distinction in the First World War and was severely wounded.

Four

The Changing Face of Town and Village

How they have changed! The photographs in this chapter illustrate very graphically how things have changed in the country and in country towns. Perhaps the most striking feature is the lack of traffic, just imagine walking up the middle of Broad Street these days, pushing a baby in a perambulator! Even strolling through the villages has its dangers today as motor vehicles whiz round corners, and, of course, new building means that all towns and villages have changed almost beyond recognition in recent times.

Broad Street, Launceston in 1890. Note the lack of traffic and a lady pushing a perambulator in the road!

Looking down Windmill Hill to Moffat's Tenement (left), now the offices of Peter and Peter, solicitors, and the Westgate Inn, c. 1905. The holly tree shown still flourishes in the gardens of Peters' offices.

Dunheved Road, c. 1865.

Dunheved Road, 1865. The left hand side of the road is now built upon and the right hand side is the present day site of the Court buildings and the Miller House residential home.

The Jubilee Inn at the top of Castle Street, with Northgate Street on the right. All this has completely changed today with Northgate Street now a pedestrian walk way and the Jubilee Inn long gone. This photograph dates from the early 1900s and the Jubilee Inn actually closed on 13 December 1909. The building later housed several families.

St Thomas Hill, c. 1910. It has not changed a great deal to this day.

Opposite above: Northgate Street in 1932. This photograph was taken prior to the so-called 'slum clearance' in 1964.

Opposite below: The Town Hall and Guildhall with the Hender Memorial Fountain, c. 1905. This photograph was taken prior to the removal of the fountain for a new road layout in the 1980s. The railings were removed in the Second World War when all iron was taken to help make munitions for the war effort.

NORTHGATE STREET, LAUNCESTON.

Launceston, Guild Hall Square.

Above: Guildhall Square with the Hender Memorial Fountain in the early 1900s. After the fountain was removed it was dumped, in pieces, in the Bangors Quarry council rubbish tip. In the 1970s the Launceston Old Cornwall Society salvaged what pieces of it were still left intact and set them up beside the reservoir at Windmill, where it is now preserved by South West Water. The building next to the Guildhall was demolished and the Conservative Club now stands on the corner site. The buildings facing and beside the castle were later occupied by Stags, estate agents and Going Places, travel agents.

The Abbot's Bridge (wrongly known locally as the Packhorse Bridge) at St Thomas, 1920s.

Above: St Leonards Bridge, near the site of a medieval leper colony, pictured here in 1860.

Opposite below: Newport Square, c. 1928. Note the calf transported in a horse and cart at the foot of St Stephens Hill! The shop front of Doidge's saddlery shop has now been demolished and the building is a private dwelling.

Above: St Thomas' Bridge, Launceston, 1930s.

Left: The chain bridge, sadly just a memory.

Above: St Stephens seen from the top of the church tower, 1930s.

Below: Launceston seen from St Stephens. Eagle House, now a hotel, is prominent on the far right.

Launceston from S. Stephens.

Pendruccombe. Formerly home of Sir Hardyng Gifford, later a school, then a private dwelling and now a residential home for the elderly.

The Jamaica Inn, made famous in the novel by Daphne du Maurier, as it was in 1934. It has since been much modernised.

Werrington Park, as shown on an engraving dated 1833.

Werrington Park and House in the 1930s and now home of Mr and Mrs Michael Williams and family.

The sixteenth-century Dockacre House, the oldest house in Launceston, as it was in 1908.

Dockacre House in 1934. It is famous for its hauntings and there are several legends attached to it.

Polapit Tamar House, Werrington, 1940s. It was built by the Coode family and was their home for many years. The Coode family were great benefactors to Werrington church.

Polapit Tamar in the 1930s. In the years after the Coode family left it became a hotel and then housed a school evacuated from the south coast during the Second World War. It is now converted into flats.

The gardens at Polapit Tamar, c. 1941.

The South Petherwin Church before the First World War. This picture was taken before the war memorial was erected in the foreground.

The Terrace, Yeolmbridge in the 1900s.

Milltown Road, Yeolmbridge in the 1900s. The house on the right was formerly the Blacksmith's Arms public house, now the home of Mr and Mrs K. Battin.

Boyton village showing the road that goes down to Boyton Bridge, 1905.

Above: Boyton village in the early 1900s. The Pound House on the right has long gone and there are a number of modern houses and bungalows now lining the road. The Methodist chapel on the left remains unchanged.

Opposite above: A view of St Keria's Church, Egloskerry in the early 1900s. The elm tree and church cottage have both now gone.

Below: Penheale Manor, Egloskerry in 1870. This beautiful house, possibly of fifteenth-century origin, was at the time of the photograph, seat of the Speccott family, but is now the home of Mr and Mrs James Colville. It retains many of its original features.

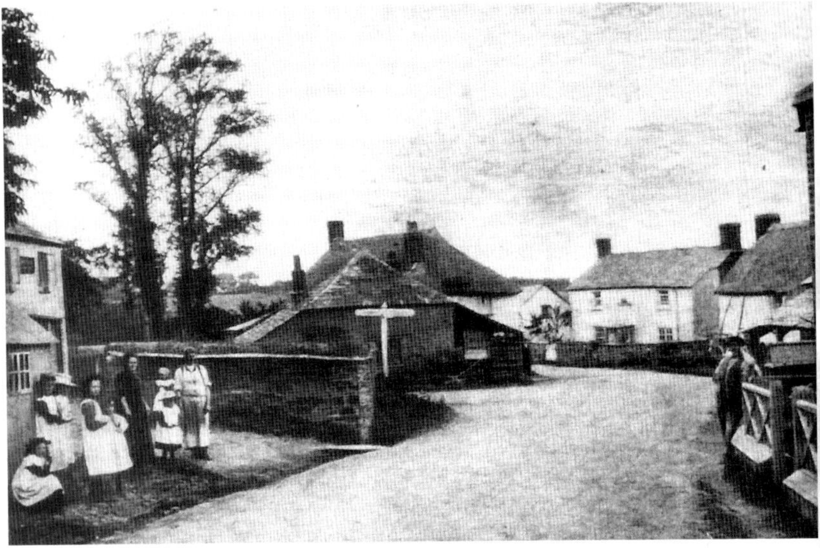

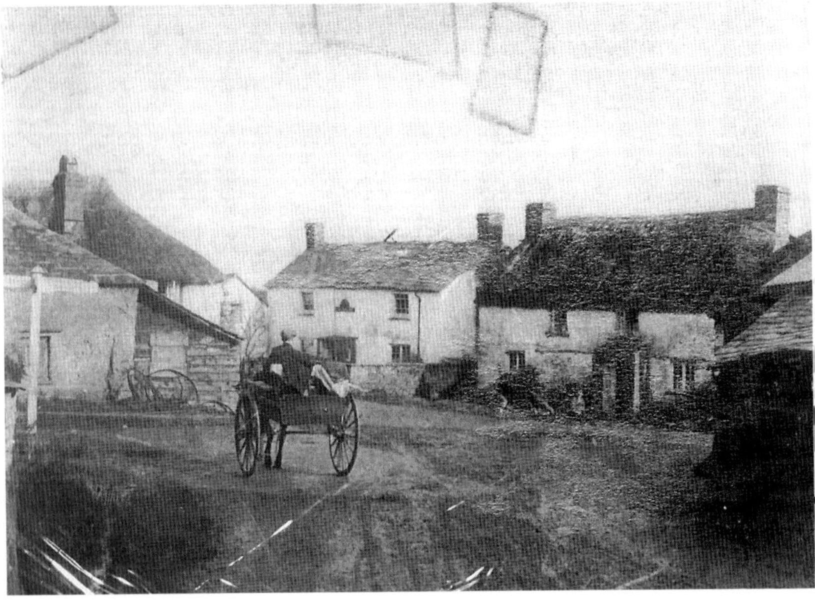

The Square, Launceston in 1910.

Opposite above: North Petherwin village in the early 1900s. The thatched cottage on the corner has long gone.

Opposite below: North Petherwin village in the 1920s just prior to the demolition of the thatched cottage and other buildings on the right.

Market day, Launceston in 1908. The Upper Market House, known as the Butter Market, was demolished in 1920-21 before the erection of the war memorial on the site. Prior to the building of the Upper Market House the Assize Court stood on the site and was demolished to make way for the market building.

Opposite above: The Square, Launceston in the 1930s.

Opposite below: The Launceston Priory ruins in the 1930s. Many of the stones of the Augustinian Priory have since been plundered and the site is very overgrown and plans have been mooted to improve it.

Launceston, The Priory.

Above: The author stands on St Leonards Bridge in the 1940s.

Left: The old almshouses at Lezant, which were demolished in 1946.

Five

The Farming Scene

Probably in no sphere of country life have things changed more than in the farming industry. The back breaking toil of yesteryear has given way to the labour saving use of modern technology, tasks are completed far more speedily than of yore and the modern farmer has to be something of a technical expert as well as a 'man of the soil'. Unfortunately, modern methods mean that a lot of the old togetherness has vanished, no longer is sheep shearing day a social occasion for wives and families as well as those actually engaged in the work, no longer do farmers have to recruit all available labour from their friends and neighbours to help them bring in the corn harvest and no longer does the beautiful scent of newly mown hay waft across the fields as it dries out in the sun. The picturesque, if hard, side of farming has gone. The photographs in this chapter may help to bring back some memories of it.

Corn harvest at South Petherwin. The horse-drawn binder bound the sheaves and threw them out ready to be stooked.

Threshing on Mr Facy's Rockwell Farm at Yeolmbridge, c. 1910.

Threshing at Rockwell, c. 1910.

Sheep shearing day at The Barton, North Petherwin, c. 1910. This was always an 'occasion' and neighbouring farmers brought sheep for shearing at the one venue.

Mr Owen Jenkin's threshing team at work in South Petherwin, 1940s. With the advent of combine harvesters the threshing team gradually disappeared from the rural scene. Threshing day was always an important one in the farm calendar. The thresher was booked well in advance and neighbours often came to help. The women folk were busy preparing food for the threshing team, taken out for them to eat where they were working.

Bull's Platt in 1910. Sheep shearing day at The Barton, North Petherwin was a big social event and wives and families turned up to watch the proceedings.

Cattle market day in Launceston. Tuesdays at the market in Race Hill were hectic and the market was always crowded. The market closed down on 18 June 1991 and the auctioneers moved operations to Hallworthy, between Launceston and Camelford. The Launceston cattle market is now a car park.

Six

Occasions

They were splashed all across the local paper when they happened and people often turned out in their hundreds to witness or take part. Some of them are still remembered but many are forgotten today. Some of the following photographs may help to jog the memory.

The exact nature of this event is not known. The photograph was taken in 1908 and it has been suggested that it was either Mayor Choosing Day or the announcement of results of an election, outside the Town Hall.

Above: The opening of St Stephens church room in 1908. The hall is still much in use for church and other functions and has been considerably modernised over the years.

Left: The dedication of the war memorial at Egloskerry in 1920.

Beating the Bounds in Launceston, here the party makes a refreshment stop. Mr Hoskin, mayor at that time, with his wife and grandson Herbert, are in the centre of the picture. Second from right is Mr Tom Sandercock, later to become Launceston's popular traffic warden and made an Honoured Burgess of the town for his services. Also pictured, amongst others, are Mr S. Fitze, Mr G. Gynn, Mrs B. Mules and Mrs Hillman.

An army recruiting team at Yeolmbridge in 1915. The barn shown on the right was later replaced by Yeolmbridge clubroom and the building on the left was demolished.

The town clerk Mr Stuart Peter reads the proclamation of King Edward VIII at Newport Square on 23 January 1935. Pupils from St Joseph's Convent school attended and standing behind the policeman is Mrs Sandercock of Roydon Road.

Egloskerry Home Guard members pose in full uniform for the first picture soon after their formation in the Second World War.

Boyton Methodist Band of Hope on Chapel Anniversary Day.

Yeolmbridge Methodist Band of Hope at Anniversary Day celebrations, c. 1900. Bands of Hope always had their instrumentalists, some could even muster a whole band. Mr Benoy stands in the centre of the back row.

Seven

Sport and Leisure

Launceston has always had a good reputation for enjoying itself, whether in the artistic or sporting field. Massive bazaars involving literally hundreds of people used to take months to organise. Pageants were popular and the school play was one of the highlights of the year. Now more sophisticated forms of entertainment have taken their place. In sport, Launceston still has flourishing football teams, especially the town team, The Clarets and likewise the Rugby Club produces many county players. There were probably more football in the old days, when almost every parish had its own team. Cricket is still very popular (Launceston was a pioneer in popularising cricket in Cornwall) but tennis has dropped somewhat in popularity. They may not be Arsenal or Manchester United but all the teams in the following photographs were proud of their prowess and they never let their town or parish down.

Prout's Motors' fleet of charabancs loaded and ready to leave The Square on an outing in 1907. It is believed to be St Mary's church Sunday school annual outing.

Egloskerry School annual outing in the 1930s.

Egloskerry School outing in the 1930s.

Egloskerry School outing in the 1930s.

Egloskerry School outing in the 1930s. On the right Mr Stan Wooldridge, driver of one of his father's firm's charabancs.

Conservative Party fete in the Castle Green in the 1930s. All the stall holders were dressed as milkmaids.

Japanese bazaar in the castle grounds, 24 and 25 June 1903. There were 14 stalls and the marquee in which they were sited was designed to represent a Japanese street with all the stalls representing Japanese cottages. The event was organised in aid of St Mary Magdelene parish church organ fund and the Additional Curates Society. The bazaar was open until 10 p.m. on both days and there were over 150 stall holders, all dressed in Japanese costume.

St Stephen's Sunday school play in the late 1920s.

St Stephen's Church Girls' Friendly Society annual outing at Crackington Haven, 1930.

St Joseph's Convent School play in the 1920s. Among those pictured is Miss Mary Fraser, then a pupil at the school.

St Joseph's Convent School play in the 1920s.

St Joseph's Convent School play in the 1920s.

Miss Ivy Jenkin (extreme left) in Japanese costume for a theatrical performance at South Petherwin in the early 1920s.

A fancy-dress football match at Launceston in 1904. The photograph was taken outside the Drill Hall, now the Westgate Centre, a day centre for people with learning disabilities.

A carnival tableau, waiting in Castle Street to join the annual carnival procession in the early 1900s. It is in stark contrast to the elaborate lorry-mounted tableaux which take part in the carnival nowadays.

The Red Cross Cadets carnival tableau in 1948.

Junior pupils at St Joseph's Convent school perform a maypole dance in the 1920s.

Keen salmon fisherman Mr W. E. Miller displays some of his catch set up outside the White Hart Hotel, of which his father was the owner at the time of this photograph, 1930s.

A famous snooker player, Joe Davis, visited Launceston Conservative Club to give a demonstration in the early 1950s. Amongst the members of the Conservative Club are John Bale, Les Stonelake, Bill Chapman, ? McCarthy, W Hender.

St Stephen's church nativity play, 1940.

Competitors in the Lands End Rally halt for a break in the 1930s. Mr Stan Wooldridge, a regular competitor for many years, is advertising Pratt's Motor Oil.

Preparing for a floral dance in Launceston Square in the 1940s. Dancers wound around the streets in imitation of the famous Helston Furry Dance in west Cornwall.

The County Council Dairy school in North Petherwin during the First World War.

Miss Betty Godbeer (now Mrs Jenkin), who was employed by Messrs J.B. Smith and Son, test drives a new 1930s Wolseley Hornet car after it arrived at the firm's showrooms.

Miss Betty Godbeer, office clerk at J.B. Smith and Son, attended the Launceston carnival fancy-dress ball in 1930 as Miss British Betty Bedford. She designed and made her own costume.

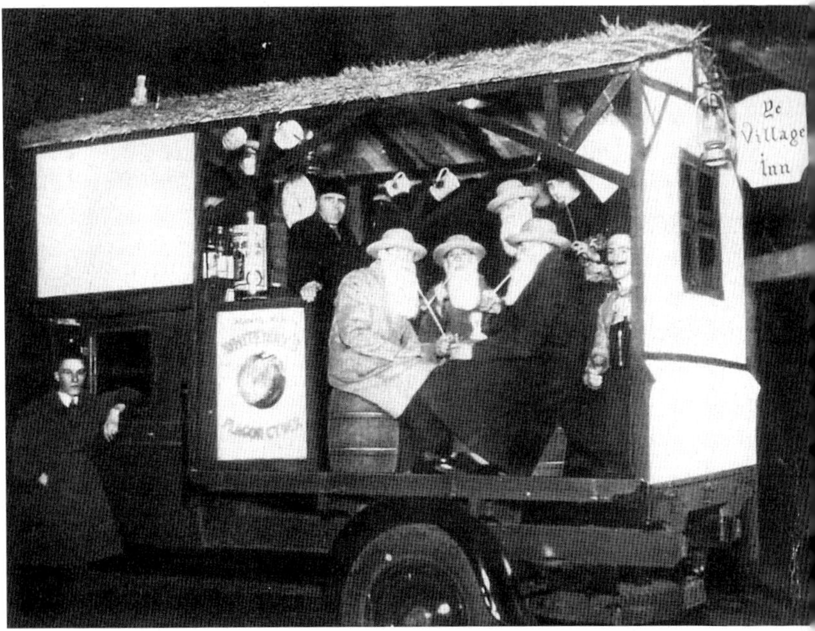
Ye Village Inn

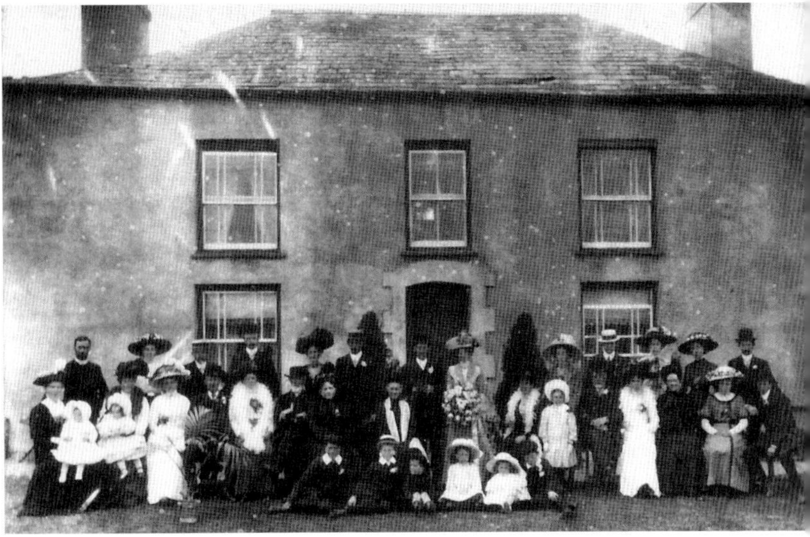

A tennis party at North Petherwin Vicarage, c. 1900. The vicarage was the only property in the parish to have its own tennis court.

Opposite above: Messrs J.B. Smith and Son's entry in Launceston Carnival in the 1930s.

Opposite below: The wedding of Mr and Mrs Ephraim Jenkin in 1909. The photograph was taken outside Westleigh House, South Petherwin.

Team members of the Devon Border Football Club pose with the Revd Trenttham, vicar of North Petherwin in the 1906-7 season. The team was mainly comprised of young men from North Petherwin.

Team members of the Launceston Football Club in the 1935-6 season.

Playing football on the sports field at Launceston College in the 1930s.

The Comrades Football Club, Launceston, in the 1919-20 season. The team was comprised of ex-servicemen who had fought in the First World War.

Launceston AFC in 1904.

Eight

School Life

What is there to say about school life in the olden days? The clothes and the rows of solemn little faces speak for themselves. Discipline was paramount, reading and writing skills taught with almost frightening intensity but most of these children emerged from their school years literate and ready to go straight into employment. We all know how things have changed, there is no need for explanation.

Werrington School pupils, 17 November 1900. Headmaster Mr B. T. Vanstone stands to the left.

North Petherwin (Brazzacott) School girls' class in the early part of 1900.

North Petherwin (Brazzacott) School boys' class in the early part of 1900.

Launceston Council School pupils in the early 1900s.

The infants' class at Werrington School in 1929.

Miss Mabel Maddever with her class at South Petherwin Primary School in the 1940s. Miss Maddever later taught in Launceston and was a very popular teacher and charming lady. She is now in her nineties but is still keenly interested in local life and especially the doings of her former pupils.

St Stephen's School infants class, 1930s.

North Petherwin Council School pupils in the 1930s.

North Petherwin Council School pupils in 1935.

Egloskerry Council School pupils in 1935.

Werrington Council School pupils in the 1930s. The headmaster, Mr B.T. Vanstone is in the centre of the back row. Freda and Kathleen Prout are in the centre of the middle row and Elsie Werren is second from the left in the front row.

Egolskerry School Group, c. 1910. The school was then held in the church hall. The group includes Archie Pike.

Werrington School pupils in 1935. Mr Frank Grant the headmaster is standing at the left of the back row.

Pupils at the National School, Launceston, c. 1940.

105

The North Petherwin School pupils, teachers and governors, 1960s. Headmaster Mr Mincher is seen centre back and next to him is Mrs Mincher. On the far left is Mrs Walter Hawke and Mrs G. B. Smale is standing in the back row.

Nine

Church and Chapel

The number of places of worship in Launceston has fallen slightly over the years and some chapels in country areas have closed. However, each parish retains its parish church and the churches and chapels in Launceston itself continue to hold quite large congregations. Some things have changed and some have stayed the same. Nativity plays in both church and chapel have altered little over the years, but Bands of Hope no longer exist and have been replaced by groups which relate more to modern life. On the whole the tradition of both church and chapel in the Launceston area is well maintained although it no longer attracts young people in the way that Bands of Hope and similar organisations did earlier in the century.

The church army caravan visits Egloskerry, c. 1900. Included in the photograph are: Mr Davis (school master), Mr Burford Snr, Mr and Mrs Strong, L. Brown, E. Lane, Ginger Gloyn, Mrs Field, Canon Drewe, Revd Swinnerton, the church army driver and the church army mission officer.

The re-hanging of St Stephens church bells in 1923. Six of the bells were cast in 1779 by the Pennington family. In 1923, Taylors of Loughborough added two new trebles to the originals which they had re-cast. All the bells have inscriptions which include: 'To the glory of God, 1923' and 'On Earth Peace, 1923'. The group are, from left to right: R. Browning, N. Tickle, H. Wickett, W. Dew, C. Tickle, W.H. Sandercock, R. Sheen, C. Birch (warden), F. Martin, C. Lampey, Cmdr. Watts-Russell (church warden), C. Paul, T. Paul, B. Wilberforce, J. Barrett, F. Paul, R. Bently, T Sandercock, W. Batten, C. Towl, G. Biddlecombe.

Launceston Baptist chapel in the early 1900s.

THE INTERIOR

WESLEYAN CHURCH, LAUNCESTON.

HARVEST HOME

A young male adults' Bible class at the Boyton Methodist chapel. The photograph was taken just after the opening of the chapel in 1899.

Opposite above: Launceston Wesleyan chapel, (now the Central Methodist chapel) with its ministers, c. 1900. The chapel has been completely modernised in recent years and is now one of the finest in Cornwall. The spire, a familiar Launceston landmark, was demolished a few years ago after becoming dangerous and too costly to repair.

Opposite below: The Middlewood chapel, North Hill decorated for a harvest festival.

Boyton Methodist chapel young female adults' Bible class, also pictured just after the opening of the chapel in 1899.

Boyton Band of Hope banner dating from 1899. With the dissolution of the Band of Hope it was displayed in the chapel in 1989.

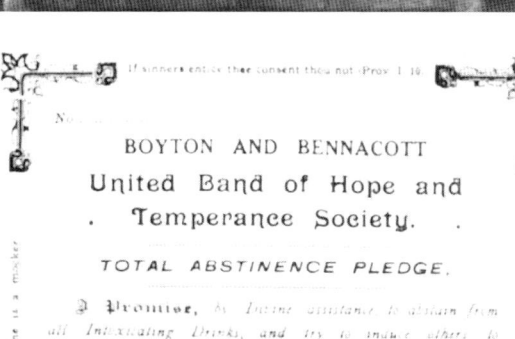

BOYTON AND BENNACOTT

United Band of Hope and

Temperance Society.

TOTAL ABSTINENCE PLEDGE.

I Promise, by Divine assistance to abstain from all Intoxicating Drinks, and try to induce others to do the same.

Signed

Witness.

Date   19

Be thou faithful unto death. — Revelations ii. 10.

A copy of the Boyton Methodist chapel Band of Hope abstinence pledge in the early 1900s. All members of the Band of Hope made this pledge.

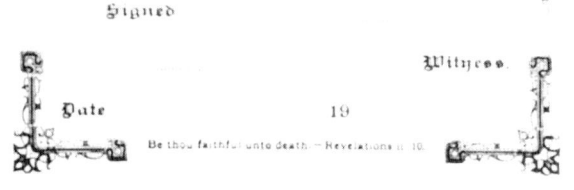

SPRING QUARTER, 1933.

The Methodist Church.

Directory and Plan

OF THE

Launceston Wesley Circuit.

January 8th to April 2nd, 1933.

CIRCUIT MINISTERS:

Rev. George A. Vernon, Treviscoe, Launceston.
Rev. H. Walker Price, Bodeglos, Launceston.

Price: THREEPENCE.

SPECIAL NOTICE.

This is the last Plan in this form. Without one opposing vote, the Local Preachers' and Quarterly Meeting have decided to issue **One Plan for the Two Methodist Circuits in Launceston.**

"Above all things put on love, which is the bond of perfectness. And let the peace of Christ rule in your hearts, to the which also ye were called in one body."—Col. 2, 14-15.

BRIMMELL BROS., PRINTERS, ETC., LAUNCESTON.

The last plan of the Launceston Wesleyan circuit, 1933.

Ten

Around and About

This chapter contains photographs which arrived too late for inclusion in earlier chapters. They illustrate the diversity of interests in town and country in days gone by and even in modern times. Dress may have changed but the spirit is the same.

Corn harvest time on Messrs E. Jenkin and Son's farm at South Petherwin, c. 1890.

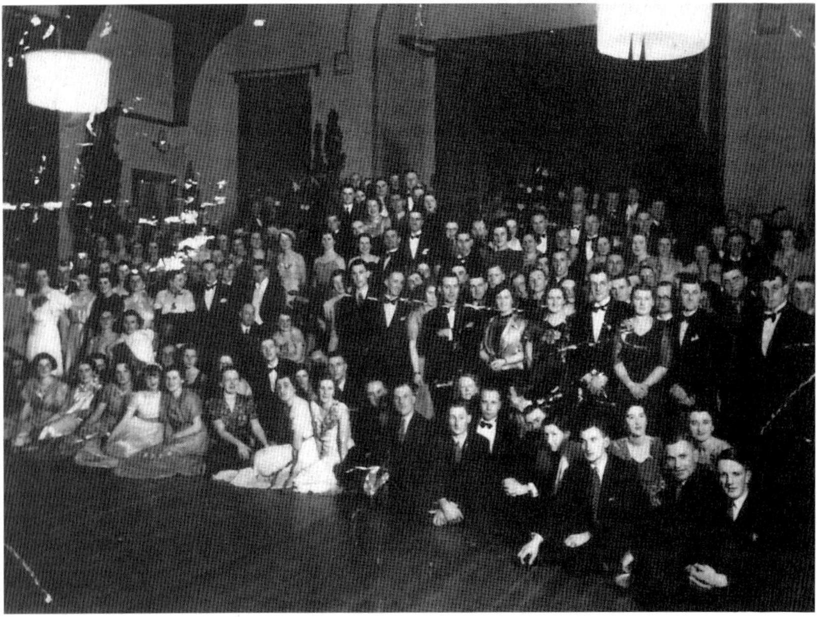

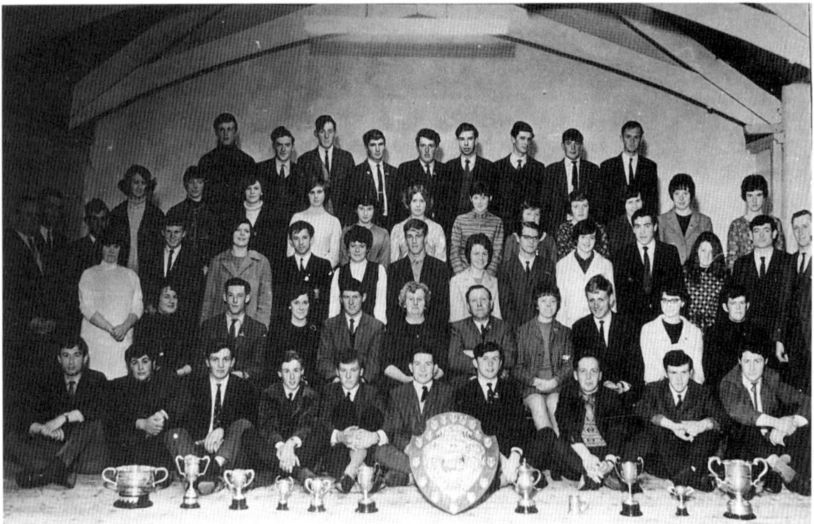

Above: The late Mr Russell Horrell was the village blacksmith at Boyton for a great many years.

Right: The late Mrs Phyllis Manning's father was a chimney sweep who used to walk miles into the country to ply his trade. Here he is at Yeolmbridge, standing on what is now the busy B3254 road. The bridge, mill and Terrace can be seen in the background.

Opposite above: The Launceston Young Farmers' Club dinner held in the town hall in the 1950s.

Opposite below: Launceston Young Farmer's Club members show off trophies won by the club. Fourth from the right in the third row is Mr Neil Burden and next to him Miss Ruth Mann. The couple are now husband and wife and have daughters of their own in the age group in which they are pictured here.

Left: An old time workman at Penheale. He carries a mole trap in his left hand and either a tree branch lopper or a tool for digging out moles in his right hand.

Below: The Board of Guardians of Pages Cross Workhouse, Launceston in the 1930s. Mr N. Heard is seventh from the left in the back row.

Opposite above: The couple is believed to be Mr and Mrs Reed of North Petherwin.

Opposite below: The Castle Temperance Hotel horse bus used to take guests at the hotel to and from Launceston railway station. The Castle Temperance Hotel horse bus used to take guests at the hotel to and from Launceston railway station.

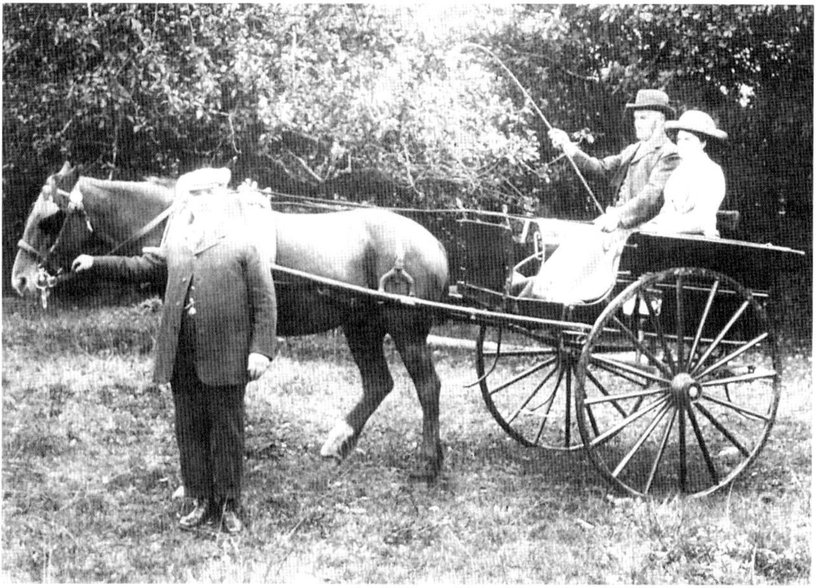

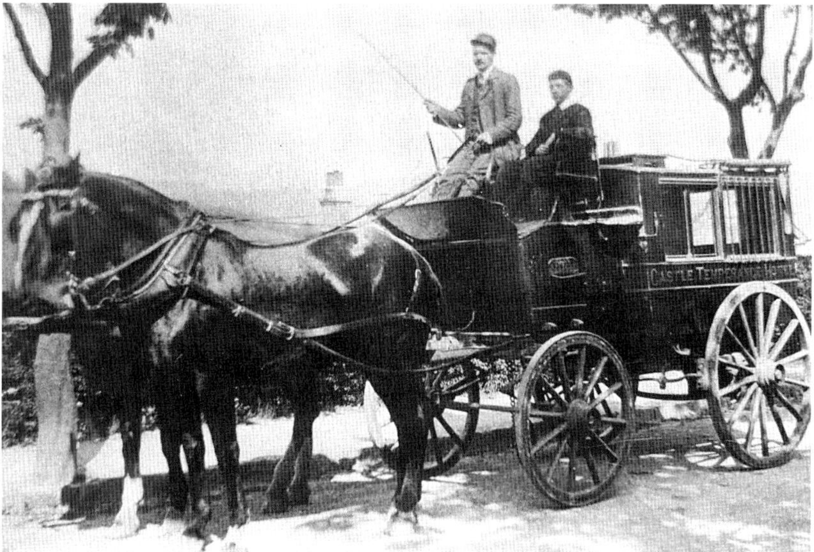
CASTLE TEMPERANCE

Left: In 1990 Mr Ronald Dinner published a book of poems dealing with his reminiscences of his service in the army during the Second World War. Entitled *A Khaki Klad's Kaleidoscope*, it proved very popular locally where Mr Dinner is well-known as a local businessman and Methodist lay preacher.

Below: Yeolmbridge Post Office closed for good in 1995 and is greatly missed by residents. Here in happier days long before closure, postmistress Mrs Barbara Body says goodbye to one of her regular customers, Mr F. Sandercock.

Opposite above: Launceston and District WI market has been a popular Tuesday event for shoppers for many years. This picture shows its early days in the town hall with Mr Bert Wyatt serving Mrs H. Kinsman at the garden produce stall.

Opposite below: St Mary Magdalene church choir, c. 1900.

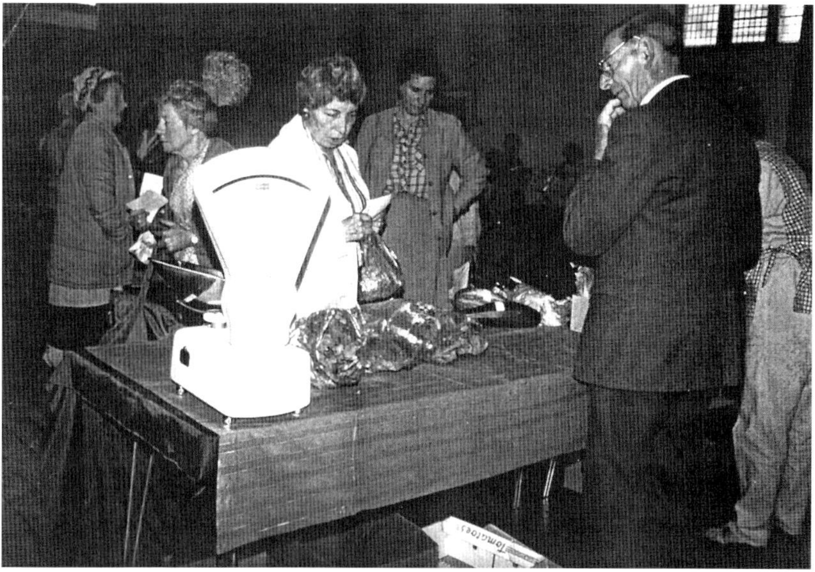
Tomatoes

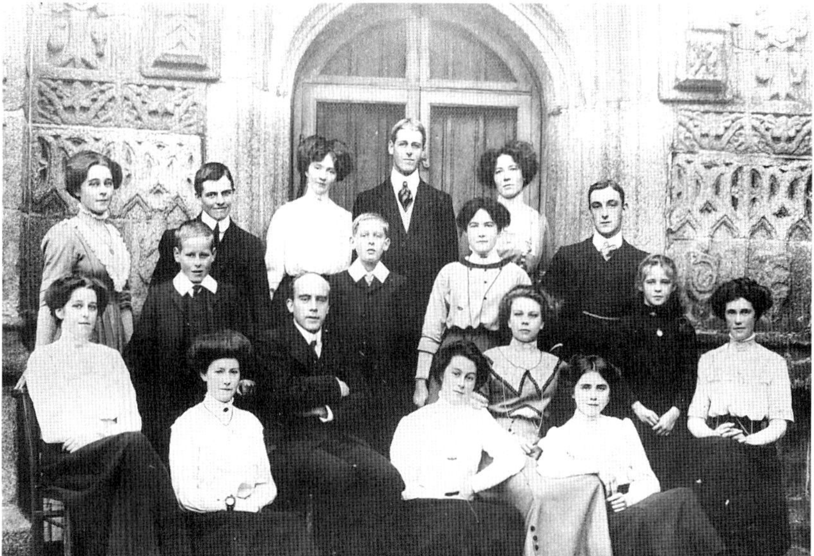

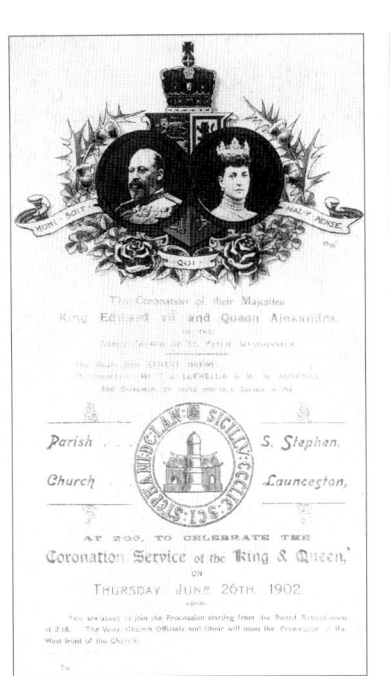

Above left: St Stephens' church programme of events for the Coronation of King Edward VII in 1902.

Above right: Sir John Speccott of Penheale, Egloskerry who was the High Sheriff of Cornwall in the reign of James I. Penheale is now the home of Mr and Mrs James Colville, Mrs Norman Colville lives in the dower house on the estate.

Opposite above: In the 1980s, members of the Central Methodist chapel re-enacted John Wesley's visit to the area and here a party is seen greeting 'Wesley' at the South Gate. The group includes Mr and Mrs Sidney Bennet, Mr Stanley Davey and Revd Martin James.

Opposite below: Bishop Peter Mumford, the Bishop of Truro, visits St Martin of Tours church, Werrington in 1988. Back row: Mr G. Dell (churchwarden), Mrs Margaret Brookham (churchwarden), Mrs Mary Brookham (PCC secretary). Font row: Bishop Mumford, Revd Allan Brownridge (vicar), Mrs Mumford, Mrs Brownridge.

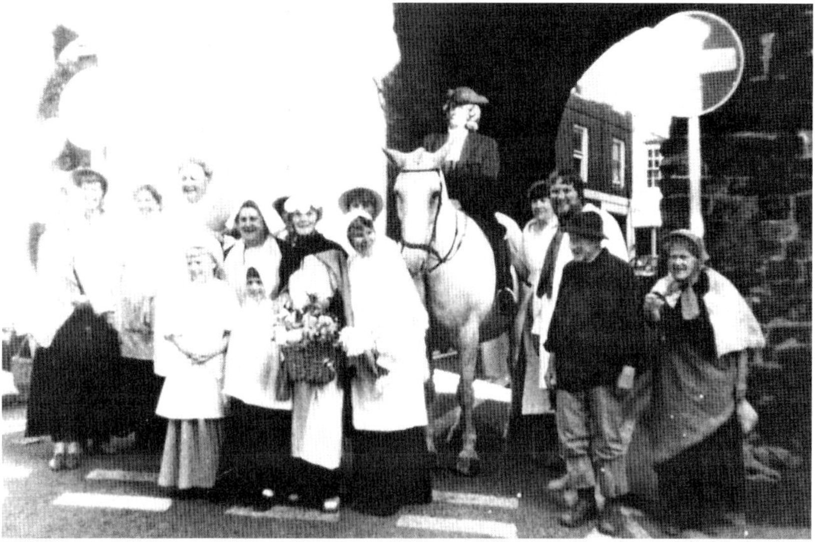

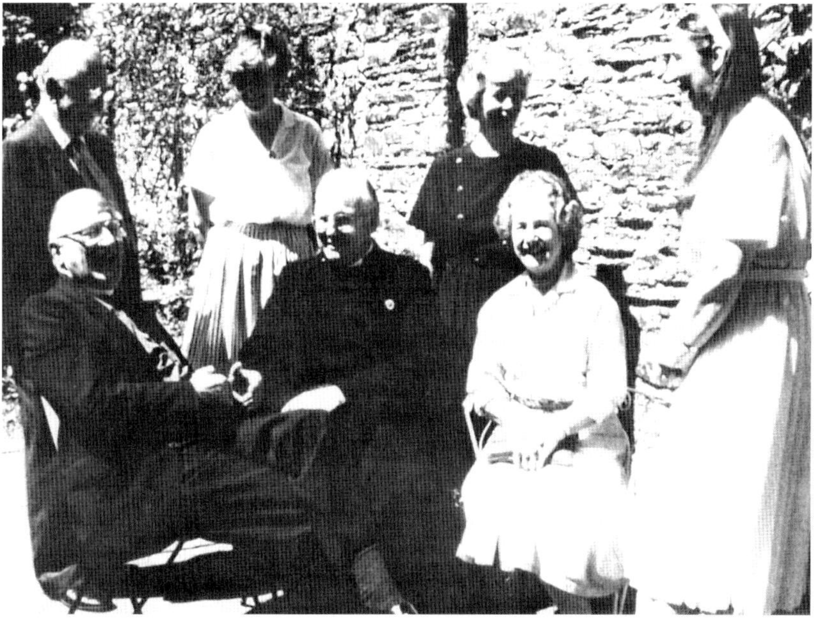

Above: Bishop Graham James, the Bishop of St Germans, visits St Giles-in-the-Heath church for a confirmation service in August 1995. He is pictured with church officers and confirmation candidates. Left to right: Mr R. Trusler, (churchwarden) Mr and Mrs Lindsay Ellacott (candidates), Lorna Gerry (candidate), Bishop James, Mrs Shopland (candidate), Tristran Gynn (candidate), Andrew Gerry (candidate), Mrs Elizabeth Thorne (churchwarden). Back row: Revd Allan Brownridge (rector), Mr Tony Black (lay reader), Claire Thomas (server).

Left: No.1 Westgate Street, now Philip Warren and Son's butchery shop, was formerly Dunn's, the grocer's, c. 1899.

Opposite above: St Thomas Hill (Old Hill) in 1900.

Opposite below: St Thomas Hill, c. 1900. Note the lack of houses in the background, an area which is now built up.

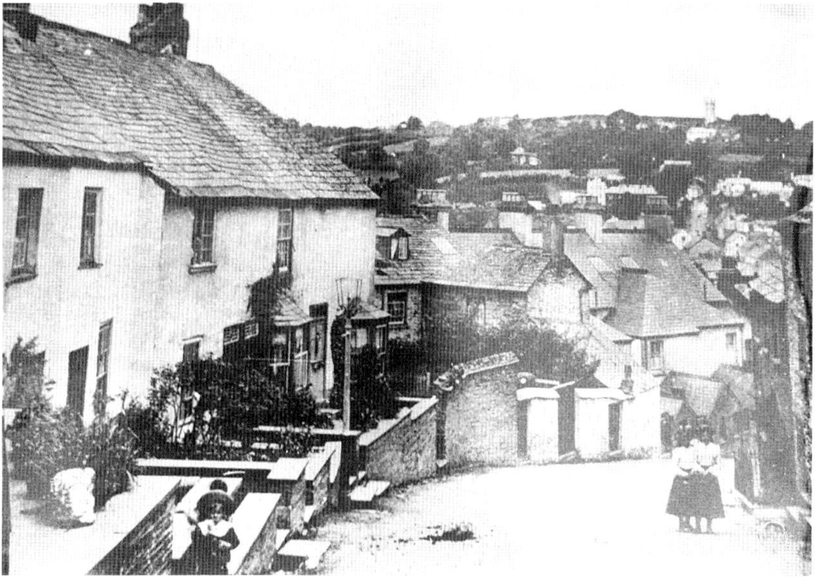

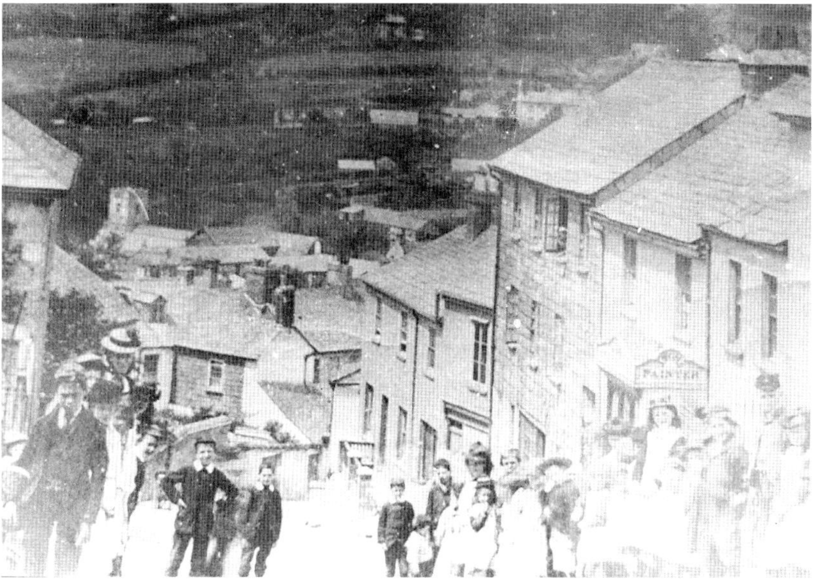
PAINTER

Launceston St. Thomas's Bridge.

THE VILLAGE

Right and below: Launceston castle under snow in 1947, one of the severest winters on record in Cornwall.

Opposite above: St Thomas Bridge in the early 1920s.

Opposite below: Sheep are driven at Petherwin Gate in 1901. Nowadays sheep are transported by lorry when they have to travel any distance. There has been so much residential building at North Petherwin that farmers seldom drive the sheep or cattle on the roads now.

Acknowledgements

When this book was first mooted my own collection of old photographs and postcards formed the nucleus but it was soon apparent that the help of friends must be sought to augment the selection of pictures to be presented. I am grateful to all those who lent precious photographs for reproduction and most especially I should like to thank the Lawrence House Museum in Launceston and its curator Mrs Jean Brown for making the recently acquired Brimmell collection available to me, and to Mr Frank Greenwood for so patiently helping me to sort the glass plates from which the selection was made. Also I thank most warmly those friends who have provided pictures: Mrs Mary Chapman, Mr and Mrs Terry Duke, Mrs Sylvia Duke, Miss Mary Fraser, Mrs Mary Hawke, Mrs Helen Jacoby, Mrs Betty Jenkin, Mrs Emily Jenkin, Mrs Nancy Jones, Mrs Mabel Mills and Mrs Lavinia Werren. Their willingness to help and the fine array of pictures which they produced for my inspection is greatly appreciated, without all of them there would have been no book, so thank you one and all.

Joan Rendell